Original title:
Peachy Dreams

Copyright © 2025 Creative Arts Management OÜ
All rights reserved.

Author: Nathaniel Blackwood
ISBN HARDBACK: 978-1-80586-332-8
ISBN PAPERBACK: 978-1-80586-804-0

Aroma of Dusk

Evening whispers through the trees,
A scent so sweet it tickles knees.
A squirrel in shades of orange glows,
Wearing a crown of fuzzy prose.

Moonlit antics start to play,
As fireflies dance in bright array.
I chase the giggles of a breeze,
While ants form bands for late-night tease.

Dreaming in Orchard Grooves

Bouncing oranges roll with glee,
In a world where laughter roams free.
A rabbit dressed in polka dots,
Is DJing tunes from sunny spots.

Breezes carry silly songs,
While dancing shadows skip along.
The apples join, a merry choir,
With sticky notes of sweet desire.

Celestial Ripeness

Stars like cherries in the night,
Spill laughter as they twinkle bright.
A cosmic fruitcake in the sky,
Delivers joy as it floats by.

Grapes wear sunglasses, looking cool,
While lemons play hopscotch near the pool.
With all this fun, the moon concurs,
As giggling clouds do gentle spurs.

Honeyed Visions

Bumblebees wear tiny hats,
And join the fun with zesty chats.
A honey pot spills tales of cheer,
As dreams buzz softly in the sphere.

Waffles wave from syrup boats,
On fluffy pillows, joy floats.
Giggles rise like dough in heat,
As morning dances on the street.

Whimsy Wrapped in Warmth

In a garden where giggles bloom,
Chasing sunbeams, we dance and zoom.
Butterflies wear silly hats, oh my!
While clouds float by, like marshmallows in the sky.

We tickle the flowers, watch them sway,
Sing silly songs, in our laughter play.
The sun winks at us, a mischievous sprite,
Painting the world with colors so bright.

The Color of Sunset Hugs

Twilight whispers in shades of tangerine,
Softening the day, like whipped cream serene.
Jellybean skies make us giggle and grin,
As we pretend to be pirates chasing the wind.

We hitch our dreams to kites up high,
With jelly-filled joy, we soar and fly.
The stars blink south like playful little sprites,
While the moon giggles softly, joining our flights.

Dreams Dipped in Juicy Nectar

Sipping sunshine, dancing on dew,
We chase the giggles, oh what a view!
Honey drips from the sky like rain,
While silly shadows play a game of charades.

Gummy bears jump on trampoline clouds,
Whirling in laughter, we're part of the crowds.
Every glance is a secret delight,
Lingering like bubbles caught in moonlight.

An Embrace of Fluffy Clouds

Floating on laughter, we ride the breeze,
Chasing fluffy dreams with whimsical ease.
Cotton candy voices call us near,
As clouds tickle our toes, it's a giggly cheer.

Painted rainbows dance on the floor,
Inviting us in for a silly encore.
With a pinch of dust from fairytale lands,
We giggle together, holding fluffy hands.

In the Depth of Juicy Nights

In moonlit splendor, fruits do dance,
Their sweetness whispers, a funny chance.
A clown in the orchard, juggles bright,
Laughing as the berries take to flight.

Wobbling watermelon rolls down the lane,
While cherries giggle, feeling no pain.
Peaches in pajamas, snoozing in style,
Dreaming of laughter that stretches a mile.

Glimpses of a Flavorful Kaleidoscope

In vibrant swirls, colors collide,
Grapes wear wigs, full of pride.
A pineapple spins a tale so grand,
While oranges play in a fruity band.

Bananas slip with a comedic grace,
Tickling berries, oh, what a place!
Limes roll in laughter, can't keep still,
In this zany blend, can you feel the thrill?

Radiance of a Silken Heart

A silky embrace, like jam on toast,
A peach wears glasses, looking like a ghost.
With giggles aplenty, they waltz in pairs,
Dancing with zest, free from all cares.

Jellybeans sing on a frosty breeze,
Mangoes do cartwheels with playful ease.
A slapstick show beneath the stars,
Fruit prances about, forgetting their scars.

A Taste of Summer's Memory

In sun-kissed days, laughter spins bright,
Strawberries tossing in a foodie fight.
Lemonade rivers, flowing with glee,
While ice cream drizzles, a sweet jubilee.

A tamarind tickles, can't help but tease,
As minty fresh breezes dance through the trees.
Remembering moments where flavors unite,
In this bowl of fun, everything tastes right.

Days Drifting on Peach Petals

Floating on soft, sticky air,
Bouncing like a light affair.
Chasing shadows, sipping cream,
Life's a never-ending dream.

Giggles echo, twirls unwind,
Splashing joy, like love confined.
Sticky fingers, laughter bright,
Swirling colors, pure delight.

Luminous Dreamscapes of Delight

In the land of jelly beans,
Hopping through the candy scenes.
Bubbles burst in rainbow hues,
Silly thoughts and silly shoes.

Tickles from the warm sun's rays,
Chasing giggles through the maze.
Each step's a dance, so carefree,
Join the fun, just wait and see!

Embraced by Nature's Lush Palette

Waltzing with the butterflies,
Underneath the waffle skies.
Painted flowers, jokes so funny,
Buzzing bees all work for honey.

Sipping nectar from a cup,
Daisies nodding, don't give up.
Every color sings a tune,
As we dance beneath the moon.

The Cascade of Sweet Laughter

Down the hill, we tumble free,
Rolling like a bumblebee.
Giggles spill like fizzy drinks,
Making all the wild things blink.

Sticky situations bloom,
In our prankster little room.
Every chuckle, every cheer,
Brings the silliness so near.

Unearthed Joys in Every Bite

A fruit in hand, so juicy and round,
Laughter erupts at the sight and the sound.
Sticky fingers, a face all aglow,
Each squirt of sweetness steals the show.

With every munch, a giggle reveals,
The dance of flavors, oh what a deal!
Strawberry smiles and banana slips,
Joyful moments, we savor each lisp.

A Symphony of Colorful Whispers

Melons sing in shades of delight,
Chorus of berries, pure and bright.
Pineapples jiggle, oranges sway,
In nature's concert, we laugh and play.

Kiwis waltz with charisma so bold,
While cherries whisper their secrets untold.
Each fruit a note, in harmony fused,
With every bite, we're happily used.

Soft Fruits on Warm Cheek

Soft plums rest where sunshine dreams,
Juicy tales spill like playful streams.
Ripe peaches tease with a gentle blush,
While giggles bubble in vibrant hush.

Oh, the nectar drips, a sticky affair,
We reach for more without a care.
Sweetness tickles our laughing spree,
As fruit dances wild on cheeks carefree.

Breezy Serenades of the Season

In gardens lush, with laughter spun,
The breeze sings sweet, a fruity fun.
Caught in a giggle, ripe apples twirl,
As nature's bounty gives joy a whirl.

A berry band plays a jolly tune,
Under the watch of a smiling moon.
Crunching delights with each silly bite,
In the dance of flavors, we take flight.

Glowing Ambrosia of Tomorrow

In a world where fruits wear hats,
And squirrels play chess with chubby cats.
The juice flows like laughter on a slide,
Bouncing off clouds with joy as a guide.

Sunny days dip in a syrupy pool,
Where gummy bears teach us to drool.
Fizzy drinks dance in the bright sunny air,
As giggles turn into confetti everywhere.

The Tang of Sweet Enchantment

Bubblegum wishes float on a breeze,
While jellybean trees rustle with ease.
Giggles and grins spread wide through the park,
As parachutes drop sweets after dark.

Charming critters in a candy parade,
Twirl in delight as confetti cascades.
Lollipop lanterns glow softly in glee,
Guiding us toward pure jubilee.

Aromas from a Summer Field

Bumblebees buzz with a ticklish tune,
Dancing around like they're over the moon.
Sugar-coated daisies sway to the beat,
As we race with the breeze, feeling light on our feet.

Frolicking shadows swing in the sun,
Fruit-flavored giggles have only begun.
Whimsical winds tickle our cheeks,
As the world plays hide-and-seek.

Ripe Fantasies in a Forgotten Garden

Hidden treasure in tangled vines,
Where balloon animals dance with signs.
The grass tickles toes with half-hearted sass,
While gummy worms giggle and pass.

Butterflies wear capes, fluttering about,
Holding secret parties, no need to shout.
Pixie dust sprinkles over the scene,
As laughter grows louder, all sweet and serene.

Juicy Fantasies

In a world where fruits can sing,
Cherries dance on a fruit-flavored swing.
Lemons juggle with zesty flair,
While grapes throw confetti in the air.

Bananas sport a silly hat,
Pineapples giggle, imagine that!
Oranges tell knock-knock jokes so sweet,
In this orchard, laughter's a treat.

Watermelons dive into pools so grand,
As strawberries form a funky band.
Kiwis play games of hide and seek,
In this humorous orchard, all are unique.

So come along, don't be shy,
Join in the fun, give it a try!
With fruity friends, the joy's immense,
In these juicy fantasies, there's no pretense.

Nectar of the Night

When the stars twinkle with fruity delight,
Honey drips from the moon, oh what a sight!
Coconuts roll in mischievous glee,
While mangoes giggle, 'Come dance with me!'

The night is ripe with silly spills,
With grape juice rivers and citrus thrills.
Avocados tell tales, oh so absurd,
While tangerines chirp like they're birds.

In the nectar's glow, everyone bows,
To the laughter of fruits, they take their vows.
Slipping on juices, they giggle and sway,
In this fruity night, we frolic and play.

So raise your glass filled with sweetness divine,
Let's toast to the fruits, and all things fine!
With laughter so rich and spirits so high,
The nectar of the night makes us all fly.

Petals in the Breeze

Petals twirl in a playful dance,
Caught up in wind's whimsical chance.
Fluffy clouds wear cotton candy hats,
While daisies giggle with shy little chats.

Sunflowers wink at the buzzing bees,
And tulips sway with the lightest tease.
In a field where daisies prance and glide,
Nature's laughter cannot be denied.

Butterflies twirl with a flutter of grace,
As peonies blush in this joyous space.
With every gust, the fun comes alive,
In this garden of giggles, we all thrive.

So join the bloom in this lively spree,
Where petals in the breeze are wild and free!
Sweet scents rise like a comic refrain,
In this floral harmony, joy we'll gain.

Pastel Skies and Secret Valleys

Pastel skies brush with colors bright,
While clouds wear costumes in playful sight.
Bouncing bunnies hop with glee,
In valleys hiding pure jubilee.

Rainbows giggle behind playful trees,
Sunshine tickles with gentle breeze.
Mountains rumble with laughter so loud,
As nature wears a joyful shroud.

In secret valleys where fun takes flight,
Silly critters dance into the night.
With skies of candy, we twirl with cheer,
In these whimsical lands, joy appears.

So grab a friend and take a chance,
In pastel realms, we'll laugh and dance!
With colorful dreams and giggles so wide,
In these secret valleys, happiness won't hide.

The Warmth of Sugar Tides

In a land where fruit rains don't cease,
Lollipops grow with perfect release.
The rivers flow with fizzy delight,
Sipping sunshine, oh, what a sight!

Marshmallow clouds drift lazily by,
Candy canes waving as they fly.
With giggles echoing through the blue,
Even the trees wear a sugar hue.

Embracing Nature's Palette

Colors burst like laughter in spring,
With frolicsome brush on an angel's wing.
Butterflies giggle in a swirl of hues,
Tickling the daisies with vibrant views.

A canvas bright with whimsical cheer,
Banana peels slip, and we all cheer.
Nature's prankster, the sun winks wide,
Painting the sky, what a playful ride!

Cascades of Luscious Thoughts

Waves of flavor crash on the shore,
Cherry bombs popping, who could ask for more?
Thoughts bounce like jellybeans in flight,
While giggles sprinkle like stars at night.

Banana boats sail on a caramel sea,
Life's a buffet of sweet jubilee.
Each idea blooms like a candy cane,
Cheerful surprises, just like a game.

The Dance of Soft Petals

Petals twirl in a silly ballet,
Dancing round like they've lost their way.
With puffs of laughter, they twist and sway,
Whispering secrets of a bright buffet.

In this wacky garden of giggly blooms,
Bees in tuxedos attend to their rooms.
Each flower giggles as they peep forth,
What a wild, whimsical place of worth!

Echoes of Flavorful Horizons

Beneath a sky of quirky pink,
A fruitwalk sprout, let's pause and think.
Banana hats and grape-sized cars,
Life's a circus, we're the stars.

With jellybean shoes and lemon ties,
We leap through clouds where humor flies.
Pies with giggles, cakes that sing,
In this land, everything is bling.

Riding rivers of fizzy cheer,
Mango music tickles the ear.
Silly dancing with jelly rolls,
Here, joy is the goal, it consoles.

So grab a slice of goofy fun,
In this world, we're never done.
With each bite, we savor more,
Echoes of laughter, we adore.

Bubbles in Sunset's Embrace

Bubbles float like dreams on air,
Soda streams, we laugh and share.
With fizzy pops and toasty cheer,
The sunset whispers, "Bring it here!"

Pineapple hats on cotton clouds,
Smiles as big as pancake crowds.
Candied laughter fills the breeze,
In this place, we dance with ease.

Gumdrop paths that twist and turn,
Marshmallow planets brightly burn.
Every giggle blooms like flowers,
Sweetened joy bursts forth for hours.

So let's toast to silly schemes,
Life's a party, bursting seams.
With every bubble, let's embrace,
The playful joy of this bright space.

Rapture in a Fragrant Dawn

Morning light with strawberry beams,
Scented whispers, drifting dreams.
We're in slippers made of cream,
Dancing 'round, it's all a theme.

Honey drips from every tree,
Joy spills out, come dance with me.
With cupcake sprinkles on our heads,
We bounce on clouds like playful threads.

Raspberry giggles paint the sky,
Tickled toes that leap and fly.
Each laughter note, a melody,
In this dawn, we're wild and free.

So raise your hands to peachy mirth,
In this place, we find our worth.
Together in this fragrant glow,
We wear our joy like a rainbow.

Sunlit Fields of Cherished Moments

In fields where cherry blossoms sway,
We gather memories, come what may.
Silly hats upon our heads,
With lemonade rivers, joy spreads.

Dandelions whisper jokes so bright,
We chase the clouds, pure sheer delight.
With every step, we twirl and leap,
In this space, the laughter's deep.

Waffle suns and syrup rain,
Every smile's a sweet champagne.
Giggling through the grassy maze,
Life's a show of silly plays.

So grab a partner, spin around,
In these fields, pure love is found.
Moments cherished in sunlit glows,
The heart of fun eternally flows.

Sweetened Slumbers

In candy clouds, we float and glide,
With giggles echoing, side by side.
Snoring softly, rainbow hues,
Chasing dreams in silly shoes.

Pillow fights and fluff galore,
Marshmallow dreams, who could ask for more?
We sip on laughter, sweet and bright,
As stars dance on, a whimsical night.

Blossoms Beneath the Stars

Under twinkling gems above,
We share a silly night's true love.
Petals chuckle, winds will tease,
Nature giggles among the trees.

Moonlight winks, it throws a fit,
As flowers sway, with every bit.
Bees in hats make quite a scene,
Buzzing jokes like a comic dream.

Soft Breaths of Summer

Sunshine spills with a playful breeze,
Lemonade laughter drips from trees.
Froggies hop with cheeky grins,
While ice cream melts, oh where it skins!

Fireflies flicker, a light parade,
Dancing shadows in a child's charade.
Sandcastles rise and tumble down,
As we wear seashells, laughter's crown.

Golden Dawn Serenade

Morning breaks in fruity hues,
Coffee spills on sleepy shoes.
Rabbits dance with floppy ears,
Singing tunes that tickle fears.

Toast pops up with a jaunty cheer,
Butter slides in a musical sphere.
Chirping birds join in the fun,
A day of giggles has begun.

The Harvest of Tranquility

Beneath the sun, we chase our glee,
With silly hats and wildelry.
A basket full of giggles bright,
We dance and skip from morn till night.

The trees wear coats of golden hue,
As bees break into laughter too.
We pluck the fruit, oh what a sight,
A feast of joy, pure delight!

A squirrel shakes his tail with pride,
While butterflies join in the ride.
Together, we will toast to fun,
In this sweet place, our laughter spun.

So let's rejoice with every bite,
Life's quirks and quirks make it just right.
We'll never leave, we're here to stay,
In our laughter's light, we'll always play.

Wandering Through Sugar Fields

In fields where sweetness sways in breeze,
I trip on clouds and munch on cheese.
The flowers wink with silly charms,
As I embrace life's quirky farms.

The sky's a canvas, colors blend,
One leg at a time, I skip and bend.
With candy canes growing from the ground,
I bounce around, oh what a sound!

Each sip of juice is laughter's song,
I sing along, can't do it wrong.
Chasing fluff that tickles my nose,
In this whimsical world, anything goes.

Giggles echo with every turn,
In sugar fields, my heart will yearn.
A paradise for silly creams,
As I wander through my sweetest dreams.

Ripe Reflections

A mirror made of fruit so bright,
I joke with shadows day and night.
The grapes giggle, the apples grin,
Their juicy jokes, they pull me in.

Reflections of a life so free,
With every bounce, I climb that tree.
The cherries chuckle at my plight,
While I just bask in pure delight.

I catch a glimpse, oh what a sight,
A silly face, that's pure delight.
With every blush, the berries cheer,
In this strange land, there's naught to fear.

So let's toast to mirrors made of fun,
A banquet shared with everyone.
In laughter's grip, we'll take our stand,
And spread the joy across the land.

Whimsical Fruits of Fancy

In gardens where the laughter grows,
A fruit that dances, everyone knows.
With fickle flavors, sweet and bright,
Each bite an echo of pure delight.

The berries gossip beneath the moon,
While joking critters dance to tune.
A watermelon with a silly hat,
Swaying along with a feathery cat.

The apples juggle, oranges gleam,
Together they form the silliest team.
With every nibble, smiles expand,
In this land of fancy, hand in hand.

In whimsical dreams, we laugh and play,
To taste the joy, it's here to stay.
With fruit of laughter and humor so bold,
Our hearts grow warm in this world of gold.

Warmth of Sunlit Contours

In the shade of a giant peach,
Beneath the giggles of a beach.
Sunshine dances on my nose,
As silly laughter freely flows.

Bizarre hats on all my friends,
With wiggly toes, the fun transcends.
We chase the bubbles in the air,
As fruity scents mingle and share.

A picnic spread with food so bright,
Ridiculous sandwiches take flight!
With each delight, we munch and munch,
And talk of dreams with a fruity crunch.

Blossoms burst in colors bold,
Their laughter wraps, a warmth to hold.
With every giggle, time does sway,
In this orbit of joy, we play.

The Blooming Essence of Daydreams

In a land of jello mountains,
With rivers made of fizzy fountains.
We skip on clouds, forget our woes,
While gummy bears dance in rows.

Twirling in the afternoon glow,
Silly thoughts start to overflow.
Like candy canes stuck in a tree,
Life's absurdity sets us free.

Over rainbow bridges made of fun,
Chasing shadows that love to run.
Each tickle from the sun's embrace,
Paints a smile on every face.

With cherry giggles echoing wide,
We ride the waves, all thoughts aside.
Finding magic in the absurd,
Daydreams bloom like laughter heard.

Blissful Threads of a Soft Dawn

Morning yawns and stretches wide,
As sleepy heads fall from their pride.
A cat in pajamas sips its tea,
And giggles float like honeybee.

With toast that talks and coffee jokes,
The day unfolds for funny folks.
Beneath the covers, dreams collide,
In a world where chuckles can't hide.

Finding socks of mismatched hues,
Wearing patterns that amuse.
Little giggles turned to roars,
As laughter dances through the doors.

The light beams in, a playful tease,
We wobble like balloons in the breeze.
In this morning's gentle frame,
Each silly moment calls our name.

Tender Reflections in Glistening Afternoon

Afternoon sun with a giggle bright,
Reflects on puddles full of light.
We jump and splash, quite contrary,
In fishy hats, we feel so merry.

Sipping lemonade from a shoe,
Inventing games only we do.
The sky chuckles in bright delight,
As butterflies soar in playful flight.

With cake that sings and cookies that dance,
Frolic in circles, we take a chance.
Running wild like sprites set free,
In this whimsical jubilee.

Chasing shadows that twist and twirl,
In a world where laughter can unfurl.
Each moment wrapped in a dandy blur,
In dreamy giggles, we do concur.

The Sweetness of Twilight

In twilight's glow, we dance, we sway,
With giggles hiding in the fray.
A fruit-basket tumble, what a scene,
As laughter spills from the in-between.

The moon peeks in with a cheeky grin,
Inviting mischief, let the fun begin!
Colors melt with a splash of zest,
Who knew nighttime could be this blessed?

In shadows long, we play our game,
Chasing fireflies, igniting the flame.
A peachy tale with a twist of lime,
Rhythms and rhymes, we're lost in time.

So raise your glass to the night's delight,
With quirky dreams taking flight.
A fruity frolic 'neath starlit beams,
Forever tangled in silly dreams.

Slumbering in Sunset's Embrace

As the sun dips low, we steal a glance,
Dreams like candy, they prance and dance.
A silly jig on a sugar high,
Tickling clouds that giggle and sigh.

Breezes blow with a fruity twist,
The world's a canvas, can't resist!
With every brushstroke, laughter spills,
A masterpiece crafted with smiles and thrills.

In this cozy nook, we drift away,
Winking stars joining in the play.
Comets race with a plucky cheer,
Who knew night was such a frontier?

So let your dreams take that wild route,
With custard clouds, and a giggle shout.
In sunset's hug, we find our place,
As the world spins in this silly space.

Dew-Kissed Daydreams

Morning calls with a laugh and cheer,
Dew on the grass, crystal-clear.
Bouncing berries in playful rows,
Tickling toes as the day grows.

We roll in petals, soft and bright,
Chasing giggles in morning light.
Mirth and mischief in a gentle breeze,
Whispered secrets amidst the trees.

Each sip of nectar tastes like fun,
With honeyed drizzles under the sun.
A tart little dance, a zesty whirl,
With every twirl, laughter unfurls.

So join the frolic, don't hold back,
In daydreams sweet, we'll find our knack.
With dew-kissed wishes floating in air,
We weave our giggles, a playful affair.

Summertime's Secret

Oh summer days, with your quirks so fine,
Miracles bubble, like soda and brine.
Sunshine whispers secrets untold,
With ice cream giggles, it never gets old.

We race through fields, where daisies play,
With painted skies that brighten the day.
A jester's hat and a cheerful cat,
Chasing shadows, where silliness sat.

So bring on the fun, with no curfew,
Mangoes and laughter, a wild crew.
We plot and scheme in the afternoon haze,
Crafting treasures in whimsical ways.

With summertime's flair, let's dance the night,
Underneath stars that glimmer so bright.
For in this season, we're light as a feather,
Spinning tales and goofy together!

Sultry Whispers Underneath the Stars

In the moonlight, we conspire,
Juicy secrets we acquire,
With silliness and a dash,
We giggle, we laugh, we clash.

The night is ripe with silly plans,
Like two clowns forming bands,
We dance beneath the dreaming trees,
Tickled by the playful breeze.

Messages wrapped in shadows soft,
Our laughter begins to loft,
With every twinkle, jokes fly high,
While crickets sing a lullaby.

Beneath the stars, our dreams take shape,
In whimsical ways, we escape,
Where folly reigns and joy won't part,
We float like bubbles, full of heart.

Fluffy Clouds Taking Flight

Up in the sky, we chase the fluff,
On candy-coated clouds, oh so tough,
Bouncing like marshmallows in the air,
We find ourselves without a care.

Giggles burst like sunlight rays,
Twirling in a fluffy haze,
Cotton candy dreams unfurl,
Like clouds in a swirly whirl.

Silly hats and sunglasses bright,
We're clouds of laughter taking flight,
Sipping sunshine lemonade,
In this whimsical charade.

As raindrops dance, we jump and play,
In our bright, joyous ballet,
With every cloud, the fun's alive,
In this fluff-filled sky, we thrive.

Timeless Summer Serenade

Sunshine spills like golden juice,
Where every hour is a funny ruse,
We chase the ice cream truck with glee,
In our hearts, wild and free.

Flip-flops slap along the way,
Singing tunes on a sunny day,
With lemonade laughter in our hands,
We dance in our jester bands.

Picnic blankets spread so wide,
With sandwiches we cannot hide,
As ants march in a silly parade,
Our summer anthem is handmade.

Each sunset paints a timeless glow,
Where giggles wave, and breezes blow,
We'll sing our song, come what may,
In this joyous summer play.

A Dance of Silken Fruity Embers

In the kitchen, chaos reigns,
With splurges, spills, and funny gains,
A dash of spice, a sprinkle of zest,
Our culinary dreams are at their best.

Pies take flight on swirling gleams,
While jammed together in silly dreams,
Fruity giggles as we stir,
In this creamy, dreamy blur.

Spoons become our shiny wands,
As we create with whims and bonds,
Muffins pop, and laughter roars,
With every batch, that joy explores.

Fruity embers ignite the fun,
In a dance where all are one,
With every bite, our hearts are light,
In this festive, fruity flight.

Mirth in the Orchard's Breath

In fields where giggles bloom,
Laughter dances in the breeze,
Fruit bats flutter 'round the room,
A jester climbs the peachy trees.

With splashes of delight in air,
The squirrels join a merry chase,
An acorn hat, they proudly wear,
While ants perform a silly race.

The sun spills juice upon the ground,
As birds whistle a funny tune,
Each step is filled with joyful sound,
The orchard hums a festive croon.

Fairies sip on nectar sweet,
Winking as they toss a prank,
Their giggles spark with every beat,
In nature's bright and fruity prank.

Citrus Hues at the Horizon

Orange skies, like buttered toast,
A playful wink from the sun,
Lemons roll and dance the most,
While tangerines just want to run.

A parrot sports a flashy grin,
Cracking jokes with every flap,
Knocking over pearly skin,
As breakfast waits with a loud clap.

Marshmallow clouds drifting by,
Giggling at the silly birds,
Who think they're flying way too high,
Wobbling on their silly curves.

Suddenly, rain of syrup drops,
Slipping on the fruity ground,
In delicious chaos, everyone stops,
As joyful laughter spins around.

Drenched in Soft Golden Light

Glistening drops of sunlight play,
As critters frolic in delight,
Chasing shadows that sway away,
In a field of pure, sunny might.

Honey bees in buzz parade,
Wearing hats of sunflower gold,
Charting routes like mischief made,
With giggles loud and stories bold.

A frolicsome breeze sings along,
Tickling leaves and hearts alike,
While butterflies join in the song,
And ants march on a giggly hike.

Every beam of warmth and cheer,
In the orchard, all is bright,
Where joy bounces, crisp and clear,
Drenched in soft, golden light.

A Tapestry of Flavorful Dreams

Woven vines of sweet surprise,
Twist and turn in spicy dance,
With berries bright and juicy sighs,
They tease you into a silly trance.

Jellybeans sprout on candy weeds,
While marshmallows fluff the clouds,
Giggling sproutlings plant their seeds,
And laugh at all the silly crowds.

Caramel rivers flow with grace,
Where gummy bears ride on the waves,
In happy drifts, they leave a trace,
Of sugary laughter in colorful caves.

Each flavor tells a funny tale,
Of fruits that flirt and dance around,
In this land where giggles sail,
A tapestry of joy is found.

Sweet Stardust Drift

A rainbow slips on a banana peel,
Getting ready for a wobbly wheel.
Socks on my hands, I dance like a clown,
In a world turned upside down.

Giggles emerge from the candy tree,
Lollipop blossoms buzz happily.
Jellybeans tumble, roll to the ground,
In this silly place, joy's always found.

Cupcakes giggle with frosting bright,
Kites made of candy take flight.
Every moment's a prankster's delight,
Under the sky, painted with sprite.

Bubbles blow silly wishes on air,
Chasing rainbows, without a care.
In a land where laughter's the prize,
We feast on pie from the sunrise.

The Essence of Soft Breezes

Twirling leaves in a breezy waltz,
Squirrels giggle, it's not their fault.
A ticklish breeze stirs the sleepy hills,
And everyone dances, just for the thrills.

Clouds wear hats, quite a spectacle,
Chasing each other, like a merry festival.
Whispering secrets in a gentle tone,
Under a laugh, they've fully grown.

Butterflies trip on their own two wings,
Wiggling with glee, oh, the joy it brings!
Daisies gossip about their petal fads,
As bees buzz in with their colorful jads.

Every breeze a giggle in disguise,
Nature's humor keeps us on the rise.
Come join the game of light-hearted fun,
As the soft air kisses everyone.

Golden Reflections in Still Waters

The pond's a mirror, but it won't behave,
Fish make faces, oh, how they rave!
Jumping up high with a belly flop,
Creating ripples, they'll never stop.

A frog in a top hat, croaking a tune,
Dancing on lily pads under the moon.
Turtles are judges, nodding with glee,
At the ballet of bugs who agree to disagree.

Sunshine beaming, splashes of gold,
The laughter of children, a sight to behold.
A picnic is planned, sandwiches fly,
As ants join the frolic, oh my, oh my!

With every chuckle, the waters will sing,
Embracing the mischief that joy can bring.
In the stillness, hilarity's found,
Where golden reflections dance 'round and 'round.

Beneath the Fuzzy Canopy

A squirrel in sneakers roams the ground,
Chasing his shadow, twist and bound.
Under a canopy of fuzzy delight,
Every branch giggles, day into night.

The chairs are mushrooms, soft as a dream,
Mice tell stories of cheese and cream.
The wind's a joker, keeps teasing the leaves,
While the flowers play hide and seek with the bees.

Jumpy rabbits in a hopscotch game,
Lose their way, giggling in the same.
Fuzzy pink clouds drift over the scene,
While sunbeams sprinkle like a golden sheen.

Under this roof of fluffy delight,
We laugh until the stars say goodnight.
Each chuckle a note in the symphony,
Under the trees, we feel so free!

Ethereal Bounty

In the orchard, shadows play,
Silly critters dance and sway.
A clownish squirrel steals a bite,
Winking in the soft moonlight.

Honey drips from tree to grass,
Mischief swirling in each glass.
With giggles echoing around,
The fruits of laughter can be found.

A jester in the russet leaves,
Wears a crown of autumn heaves.
Sipping nectar, sweet and bright,
Chasing dreams that take to flight.

Beneath the sky, a funny scheme,
Frolics burst like a wild dream.
In this place, where joy's the king,
Even the stars begin to sing.

A Chorus of Orchard Sighs.

Among the branches, laughter flows,
Rustling leaves in silly throes.
Crickets join with squeaky cheer,
In a musical atmosphere.

Robin redbreasts start to twirl,
Chasing dew with each bold whirl.
Sweet fruit jokes are ripe to peel,
As nature's humor is revealed.

With giggling blooms so blithe and bright,
Banish shadows, welcome light.
Grapes in jest tie knots of glee,
Growing funny as can be.

The twilight whispers tales of fun,
Where silly fables intertwine and run.
In the orchard's warm embrace,
Come find your smile, your happy place.

Juicy Whispers of the Night

In the moonlight, secrets swell,
Fruits giggle, all's well.
Raspberry thorns play hide-and-seek,
While neighbors laugh, and hedgehogs peek.

Beneath the stars, a juicy prank,
An orange rolls, a toss, a spank!
Lemons cackle, tart and sweet,
For every slip, there's a treat.

Whimsical whispers float on air,
As night unfolds with silly flair.
A chubby peach starts to wink,
Making everyone stop and think.

With laughter weaving through the trees,
The fruits converse with playful ease.
In this haven where giggles bloom,
Beneath the stars, no sign of gloom!

The Sweetness of Twilight

As the sun dips, colors blend,
In the garden, fun won't end.
Berries burst in fits of glee,
Tickling all who dare to see.

A perky plum spins round and round,
While grapes tumble to the ground.
Each one brims with silly cheer,
Pouring laughter in the sphere.

With every bloom, a joke in tow,
Blossoms giggle, putting on a show.
Carrots chat with breezy grace,
Mirth and mischief interlace.

In this patch of twilight's glow,
Where winks and chuckles freely flow.
The essence of sweet, soft delight,
Creates a world where smiles alight.

Nostalgic Fruity Whimsy

In a garden where tickles grow,
Laughter blooms, putting on a show.
Silly squirrels with hats ask why,
As jellybeans leap, oh my, oh my!

Sunshine giggles upon the chair,
Marshmallow clouds float in the air.
Bouncing berries keep time with squeals,
Whispers of fruit, what joy it reveals!

Grapes in pajamas dance on the grass,
While lemon drops giggle as they pass.
A banana slips with a chuckle and roll,
In this fruity realm, we're all on a stroll!

Memories swirl like a sweet summer breeze,
Each silly moment sure aims to please.
With every bite and laughter shared,
These whimsical nights have us all ensnared!

The Lushness of Lullabies

Cuddled up in the strawberry patch,
Where gumdrop dreams are easy to catch.
Jellyfish clouds float and tease,
While nighttime whispers put worries at ease.

Under moonbeams, bouncing, we sway,
As bubblegum breezes carry away.
Sleepy lemons snore in delight,
Telling tales of sugary flight.

Cherries hum tunes of sweet serenades,
While licorice vines form sleepy cascades.
Watermelon stars twinkle and gleam,
Wrapping us softly in a fruity dream.

Laughter and joy drift on by,
In a world where the wild and sweet sky.
As night wraps around in a cozy embrace,
We float in slumber, a blissful place!

Honeyed Hopes in Gentle Breezes

Beneath the branches, hope takes flight,
A frosty mint breeze dances with the night.
Lollipops spin tales full of cheer,
While cotton candy whispers, 'Come near!'

A breeze with giggles dips and swings,
As caramel dreams wrap us in flings.
Saffron skies and orange zest smiles,
Fill our hearts with sweetened miles.

Ginger snaps jive with the honey bees,
While whistleberry songs float through the trees.
Raspberry rain showers sprinkle delight,
In a world where we twirl with pure light.

Let's waltz with joy in this realm of fun,
Chasing the day until it's done.
With honeyed wishes, we take a leap,
In the whirlwind of dreams, happiness to keep!

Luminous Fancies of the Heart

In the glow of twilight, joy will embark,
With a wink of whimsy, igniting the spark.
Sassy figs wear colorful caps,
As vibrant dreams flow in comical laps.

Mirthful dances spring from the vine,
With jelly-filled laughter, sweet as wine.
Orange twirls in the quirky breeze,
While dancing apples move with ease.

Luminous hopes leap from delight,
Swinging on swings in the soft twilight.
Pineapple antics and merry delight,
Fill the canvas of a whimsical night.

With every chuckle and every spin,
In this fruity realm, we dive right in.
Holding hands, our hearts entwine,
In the radiance of joy, ever fine!

Eyes Glazed with Sunkissed Delight

In the morning sun, I spy a treat,
A fuzzy orb that smells so sweet.
With every bite, I grin so wide,
  Juicy dribbles I cannot hide.

Laughter bubbles, sticky hands,
Sunkissed moments, cheerful lands.
Each slice a giggle, each core a cheer,
This fruity bliss is what I hold dear.

With faces smeared, we dance around,
In blissful joy, we're totally bound.
These silly smiles, a joyful scheme,
Oh such merriment, like a silly dream!

As twilight falls, my heart takes flight,
Under the stars, my soul feels light.
With dreams of joy, my heart will sway,
In this sweet world, I want to play.

Layers of a Juicy Memory

A slice of sunshine, a giggle or two,
With every layer, the fun just grew.
Beneath the skin, a treasure awaits,
Juiciness spills, oh, this one celebrates!

With sticky fingers and joyful shouts,
We craft our stories, no room for doubts.
Each bite a tale, each taste a cheer,
In laughter's embrace, we lose all fear.

The layers stack high, like happiness piled,
Making memories, oh so wild!
In this tangy delight, smiles appear,
Forever etched, year after year.

So pour me the juice, let it flow free,
A carnival of flavors, just you and me.
We'll savor the moments, both silly and wise,
In this juicy realm, our spirits will rise!

Silken Skies of Hushed Melodies

Beneath soft clouds of cotton candy dreams,
Laughter floats like gentle streams.
With a taste of sweetness, hearts take flight,
In twilight's glow, we giggle at night.

Whispers of joy in the evening air,
Fruity laughter, with none to spare.
As the stars wink down, we share our tales,
In this twilight hush, every giggle prevails.

The sky a canvas, painted with cheer,
Each note a melody that draws us near.
We sway and dance, lost in delight,
In this soft glow, everything feels right.

With skies so silken, our hearts won't roam,
In this joyous world, we've found our home.
Let laughter echo, let dreams unfold,
In these whispered moments, our joys are told.

Cradled in Gentle Euphoria

In the arms of joy, we find our way,
Sipping sunshine on a bright summer's day.
With giggles and winks, we float like a breeze,
In gentle euphoria, we do just as we please.

Soft as a peach, our spirits gleam,
Bouncing in laughter, a sweet daydream.
Silly dances under trees so grand,
In this blissful state, hand in hand.

Every giggle sparks a glimmering light,
In a world of wonder, everything feels right.
With each hearty chuckle, our souls sing free,
In this sacred space, just you and me.

So let's toast to joy, with a splash of cheer,
In gentle euphoria, we'll shed every fear.
With hearts wide open, oh how we'll play,
In this whimsical world, forever we'll stay.

Fruitful Whispers

In the orchard, laughter grows,
Bouncing fruits wear silly clothes.
A banana slips, we all chime,
As apples dance, oh what a rhyme!

A grape on top thought he was bold,
But wobbled down, the story told.
Mango jokes shared on the breeze,
Tickling cheeks with all their tease.

Peaches giggle, round and bright,
Rolling down, what a delight!
Citrus smiles in sunlight sway,
Making every frown decay.

With berry cheers, we take a stand,
Fruitful whispers, oh so grand!
Join the fun, the harvest cheer,
In this orchard, joy's so near!

Sunlit Reveries

In sunlit fields, a cherry pranks,
Swinging from the branches' banks.
A lemon slips, a jolly jest,
While peaches play, they love the fest!

Honeydew, with giggles, rolls,
While laughter sweetly fills our souls.
Cantaloupe in shades of fun,
Join the laughter, everyone!

Tangerines toss jokes around,
While grapefruit hums a silly sound.
Bananas wear their brightest grin,
As fruit parade begins to spin!

Underneath the warmest rays,
Berries make the silliest plays.
In this dream where laughter's free,
Join us in this fruity spree!

Velvet Hues of Dawn

As dawn unrolls, we wake with glee,
A pear sings songs, so joyfully.
Kiwi ghosts in playful dance,
Make us giggle at first glance!

With velvet hues, the morning glows,
As passion fruits tease with their prose.
Watermelon with a wink so sly,
Makes us laugh, oh my, oh my!

Avocado dreams in shades of green,
Telling secrets never seen.
Juicy tales and stories spun,
In this orchard, joy's begun!

So come and join the fruity fun,
With every laugh, our hearts will run.
In this dawn where giggles bloom,
Find your joy, dispel the gloom!

The Orchard's Lullaby

In the orchard, where dreams are spun,
Fruits play tricks, oh what fun!
A jester pear, with laughter bright,
Sings of joy throughout the night.

A dancing fig, with ruffled leaves,
Whispers secrets, none believes.
Grapes form giggles in the sun,
In this lullaby, all's begun!

Cider moons and plum stars gleam,
As berries weave a silly dream.
Lemons crack jokes, ever sweet,
While cherries tap their tiny feet.

So let us sway in nature's tune,
As every fruit bursts into bloom.
In this orchard, laughter flies,
Dreams take root beneath the skies!

Sun-Kissed Reveries

In fields of gold, we dance and sway,
Chasing sunbeams, laughing away.
A twist of fate in the sunlight's gleam,
Oops! I spilled my sweet ice cream.

With hats so big and shades so bright,
We pose with joy, what a silly sight!
Twirling around, we feel so free,
Watch out for that tree, oh dear me!

Blossom-Flecked Slumber

Fluttering petals tickle my nose,
As I nap under trees—their cozy prose.
A giggling breeze whispers secrets unknown,
While ants hold a dance party on my phone.

Dreams of cake in a frosted haze,
Oh, I'm covered in confetti for days!
Each fluffy cloud, a marshmallow treat,
I'll take two spoons now—make it sweet!

Summer's Silken Caress

A splash of juice from the fruit I bite,
Drips down my chin, oh what a sight!
With a wink and a grin, I wear it well,
Like a crown of citrus, can you tell?

Barbecue smoke is a savory breeze,
While my friend tries to catch it with ease.
Sticky fingers and laughter collide,
We'll take on summer, let fun be our guide!

A Slice of Morning Glow

With breakfast scents that fill the air,
I dance on toast without a care.
The coffee's strong, but not as much,
As the giggles from my morning crunch.

Eggs doing yoga, pancakes pretend,
In this silly kitchen, the fun won't end.
With maple syrup rivers to flow,
Each bite of joy—a tasty show!

Nectar in the Moonlight

Under the stars, they start to dance,
Whispers of fruit in a romping prance.
Bouncing around, in a light-hearted spree,
Mirthful laughter spills like honey from a bee.

Beneath a tree, a bright fruit shines,
Tasting sweetness through silly lines.
Squirrels giggle as they play hide and seek,
Feasting on joy, oh, what a peak!

In the cool night, dreams take flight,
With a jester's hat, everything feels right.
A splash of juice paints the whole town,
As giggles bubble up, not a single frown.

So raise your glass to the odd and sweet,
With dancing fruit, life's a treat.
In this moonlit chaos, we find our cheer,
In the nectar tonight, let's disappear!

Gentle Hues of Satisfaction

In a world of color, we paint with flair,
A splash of orange, nothing to compare.
Giggles erupt from each juicy bite,
Delightful surprises, oh what a sight!

Sipping shades of sunrise, laughter ignites,
With every sip, the silliness bites.
Toasty tints mingle, a fruity masquerade,
Each little flavor, a joyful cascade.

Dancing in circles, the fruit flies by,
Chasing the sweetness, oh me, oh my!
With pops of color like confetti from the skies,
Life's a circus where nonsense never dies.

So let's swirl like a smoothie, bright and bold,
In gentle hues, we find stories to be told.
With laughter our palette, and joy our pride,
In the art of the silly, let's take a ride!

Orchard's Lullaby

In orchards bright, where the laughter grows,
The trees tell secrets that nobody knows.
With every giggle, a branch starts to sway,
Fruits drop in rhythm, come join the play!

Breezes hum soft songs through the leaves,
While buzzing insects deliver some heaves.
A chorus of chuckles in the soft evening light,
Fruitful lullabies make everything right.

Silly shadows twist, hop and glide,
As the night wears on, shenanigans slide.
With dreams made of nectar, we drift into glee,
In the orchard's embrace, happy as we can be.

So close your eyes tight, let the jester sing,
In this lullaby land, joy's the main thing.
With fruits hanging low, and laughter so sweet,
We dance through the night on our fanciful feet!

Creamy Skies at Dusk

As the sun dips low, the skies blend and swirl,
Like creamy delights in a mischievous whirl.
Clouds giggle softly, a fluffy parade,
Painting our evenings in whimsical shades.

Time to rocket past serious sighs,
With winks and nods under cotton candy skies.
Who knew such laughter could bloom as we gaze,
At the crayon art of twilight's warm haze?

Dip into sweetness, let your spirits fly,
With every chuckle hanging in the sky.
A sprinkle of humor, a dash of delight,
In creamy concoctions, everything feels right.

So clap for the dusk in its playful attire,
With joy as our fuel, we never tire.
In the land of giggles, let's take our stands,
With lighthearted whimsy stretched across the lands!

www.ingramcontent.com/pod-product-compliance
Lightning Source LLC
Chambersburg PA
CBHW070317120526
44590CB00017B/2713